Sports Illustrated KIDS
STARS OF SPORTS

JALEN HURTS

DUAL-THREAT QUARTERBACK

by Matt Chandler

T0403251

Published by Capstone Press, an imprint of Capstone
1710 Roe Crest Drive, North Mankato, Minnesota 56003
capstonepub.com

Library of Congress Cataloging-in-Publication Data
Names: Chandler, Matt, author.
Title: Jalen Hurts : dual-threat quarterback / by Matt Chandler.
Description: North Mankato, Minnesota : Capstone Press, 2026. | Series: Sports illustrated kids : stars of sports | Includes bibliographical references and index. | Audience: Ages 8-11 | Audience: Grades 4-6 | Summary: "Jalen Hurts was a five-sport athlete in high school. He put all his focus into football and chose to play at the University of Alabama. Despite starting strong, Hurts was eventually benched. This adversity made him a stronger player and reshaped his future, taking him to Oklahoma for his senior year. In 2020, Hurts was drafted by the Philadelphia Eagles and became the face of the team. The drive and talent of Jalen Hurts is front and center in this fact-filled sports biography."—Provided by publisher.
Identifiers: LCCN 2024054066 (print) | LCCN 2024054067 (ebook) | ISBN 9798875222658 (hardcover) | ISBN 9798875222603 (paperback) | ISBN 9798875222610 (pdf) | ISBN 9798875222627 (epub) | ISBN 9798875222634 (kindle edition)
Subjects: LCSH: Hurts, Jalen, 1998- —Juvenile literature. | Quarterbacks (Football)—United States—Biography—Juvenile literature. | Football players—United States--Biography—Juvenile literature.
Classification: LCC GV939.H865 C53 2026 (print) | LCC GV939.H865 (ebook) | DDC 796.332092 [B]—dc23/eng/20241217
LC record available at https://lccn.loc.gov/2024054066
LC ebook record available at https://lccn.loc.gov/2024054067

Editorial Credits
Editors: Patrick Donnelly and Christianne Jones; Designer: Sarah Bennett; Media Researcher: Svetlana Zhurkin; Production Specialist: Tori Abraham

Image Credits
Associated Press: Brynn Anderson, 11; Getty Images: Alika Jenner, 19, Brian Bahr, 17, Chris Graythen, 24, 28, Christian Petersen, 23, Dustin Satloff, 27, Kevin C. Cox, 5, 13, 15, Maddie Meyer, 12, master1305, 1, Michael DeMocker, 25, Mike Coppola/Prime Video, 26, Mitchell Leff, cover, Ronald Martinez, 10, RoschetzkyIstockPhoto, 6, Tim Nwachukwu, 20; Newscom: Cal Sport Media/Justin Cooper, 14, Icon Sportswire/Ken Murray, 7; Shutterstock: Real Sports Photos, 9

Source Notes
Page 15, "I look up at my dad . . ." Michael Casagrande, "Jalen Hurts opens up about crying in parents' arms after title-game benching," AL.com, December 2, 2018, https://www.al.com/alabamafootball/2018/12/jalen-hurts-opens-up-about-crying-in-parents-arms-after-title-game-benching.html, Accessed November 2024.

Page 20, "good backup. . ." "Jalen Hurts," NFL.com, https://www.nfl.com/prospects/jalen-hurts/32004855-5276-7022-35cf-a74490936f42, Accessed November 2024.

Page 25, "Things come right on time . . ." Rob Maaddi, "'Eagles deny the Chiefs a Super Bowl three-peat with dominant defense," The Associated Press, Feb. 10, 2025, https://www.chroniclejournal.com/news/world/eagles-deny-the-chiefs-a-super-bowl-three-peat-with-dominant-defense-in-a-40/article_8c76de0c-5ff1-59e1-97a6-8c9e73aaa2d8.html, Accessed February 2025.

Page 27, "I was once a kid . . ." Chris Bumbaca, "'Symbol of hope': Inside Eagles QB Jalen Hurts' day giving back to Philadelphia community," USA Today, December 15, 2022, https://www.usatoday.com/story/sports/nfl/eagles/2022/12/15/jalen-hurts-eagles-qb-day-of-care-philadelphia-community/10897830002/, Accessed November 2024.

Printed and bound in China.   006276

TABLE OF CONTENTS

Words in **BOLD** are in the glossary.

THE BACKUP

It was the fourth quarter of the 2018 College Football National Championship. Alabama trailed Georgia 28–21. Alabama's starting quarterback, Tua Tagovailoa, had been injured. Jalen Hurts jogged onto the field. The backup quarterback had a chance to be the hero.

Hurts led Alabama to Georgia's 10-yard line. On third down, Hurts rolled out to his right. He fired a strike to Jerry Jeudy in the corner of the end zone. Touchdown! The game was tied.

With three minutes left, Alabama got the ball back near midfield. Hurts quickly drove his team to the 15-yard line. On first down, Hurts dropped back. But he didn't throw. He planted his foot and raced toward the end zone. Hurts beat two defenders to score the game-winning touchdown.

>>> Jalen Hurts takes a moment in the end zone after scoring the game-winning touchdown against Georgia in the championship game.

5

CHAPTER ONE
TEXAS BALLER

Jalen Hurts was born on August 7, 1998, in Houston, Texas. His mom, Pamela, has a master's degree in counseling. His dad, Averion, coached Jalen's high school football team. His older brother, Averion Jr., played football. His younger sister, Kynnedy, played volleyball. His family played a huge role in his success.

》》》 Houston is the biggest city in Texas.

》》》 Hurts with his brother, sister, and mom before a 2022 game.

Jalen's **godfather** worked for the Houston Texans. He invited Hurts to training camp and practices. Those early memories stuck with him during his football journey. While other kids were playing basketball or video games, Hurts was in his yard practicing football. He just loved the game.

FACT

Hurts learned how to cook at an early age. Crawfish and pig's feet are two of his favorite meals to make.

At Channelview High, Hurts was a five-sport athlete. He played baseball and basketball. He also competed in track and field and **powerlifting**. But football was his obsession. Playing for his dad, Hurts had a great high school career. As a senior, he led the team in passing and rushing.

He also won what he's called the most important game of his career. It was in 2014 when Channelview faced **rival** North Shore High. Channelview had never beaten North Shore. Hurts threw a last-second touchdown pass to pull off a miracle win.

Powerlifting QB

Hurts became a powerlifter because his dad thought it would help him recover from an injury. In the 2015 Division 1 High School Championships, Hurts deadlifted an incredible 585 pounds (265 kilograms). He was just 16 years old!

>>> Powerlifters have very strong arms and legs.

CHAPTER TWO
FROM ALABAMA TO OKLAHOMA

College powerhouses such as Texas A&M, Mississippi State, Florida, and Alabama all wanted Hurts to play for them. He chose the University of Alabama. He wanted to play under legendary head coach Nick Saban.

>>> Nick Saban was Alabama's head coach from 2007 to 2024.

> Hurts throws a pass in his first college start against Western Kentucky.

On September 10, 2016, Hurts started his first college game for the Crimson Tide. More than 100,000 fans packed Alabama's stadium. If the freshman was nervous, he didn't show it. He threw for two touchdowns and 287 yards, leading Alabama to a 38–10 victory.

Alabama had a perfect 12–0 regular season. Hurts led the team in passing and rushing. But after a **grueling** season, they needed two more wins to reach the national championship game.

First, Alabama faced Florida for the 2016 SEC title. The Tide won easily, 54–16. But Hurts had a quiet game. He passed for 138 yards and had just one rushing yard.

Then Alabama faced Washington. Hurts struggled against the Huskies defense. But Alabama's strong defense and solid running attack helped the Tide win 24–7.

〉〉〉 Hurts and Derrick Gore celebrate after beating Washington.

>>> Hurts tries to outrun a Clemson defender during the National Championship game.

On January 9, 2017, Alabama faced Clemson in the College Football National Championship. Hurts struggled to complete passes and missed open receivers. The Clemson defense was too much. Hurts's fairy-tale season ended with a 35–31 loss.

FACT

Hurts was named SEC Offensive Player of the Year and SEC Freshman of the Year for his incredible first season at Alabama.

Hurts returned to form in 2017. He led the Tide to another strong season. They finished 11–1 and reached the championship game again. Hurts would have his shot at **redemption**.

But the struggles of the previous year returned. He was never able to find his rhythm against SEC rival Georgia. With the Tide trailing 13–0 at halftime, Saban made a change. He brought in freshman quarterback Tua Tagovailoa. The change worked. Tagovailoa threw three touchdown passes, including the game-winner in overtime. The Tide were national champions!

》》 Tagovailoa passes for the game-tying touchdown in the national title game against Georgia.

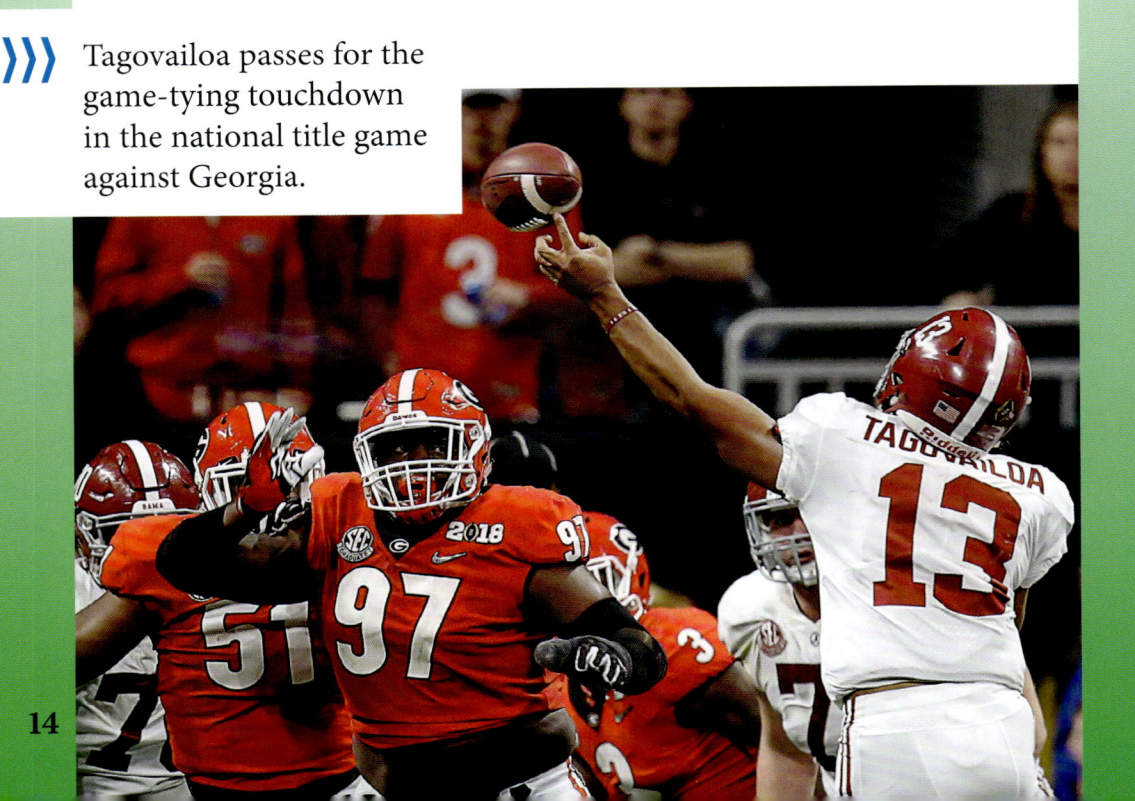

》》》 Reporters interview Hurts after he was benched in the national title game.

Hurts called that night one of the toughest of his life. His record at Alabama was 26–2, and he was benched after a bad first half. He watched his backup lead his team to victory. He cheered for Tagovailoa and celebrated with the team. Then he went back to his hotel room with his parents and cried.

"I look up at my dad and said, 'What are we going to do now?'" Hurts recalled. "He looked me in my eyes and said, 'We are going to fight.'"

Most football experts expected Hurts to **transfer** after being benched. But he didn't. He stayed and fought. Even when Tagovailoa was named the starter for 2018, Hurts embraced his role as the backup.

Hurts played in 13 games off the bench that year. The Tide returned to the national title game for the third straight season. This time, they lost to Clemson again. Hurts decided it was time to move on. He needed more playing time to prepare for a professional football career.

On September 1, 2019, Hurts took the field for his new team, the Oklahoma Sooners. He had changed his uniform number, but everything else was **vintage** Hurts. He finished his one season in Oklahoma with 3,851 passing yards and 1,298 rushing yards. He added 52 total touchdowns and led his team to the Big 12 Championship.

Hurts sprints for a touchdown against Oklahoma State.

CHAPTER THREE

FLY EAGLES FLY

Hurts entered the 2020 National Football League (NFL) Draft. So did his former teammate, Tagovailoa, who was taken with the fifth pick. Hurts waited to hear his name called. Finally, the Philadelphia Eagles selected him with the 53rd pick.

Hurts signed a four-year contract. He spent most of his **rookie** season as the backup to **veteran** quarterback Carson Wentz. But with the Eagles in last place, the rookie finally got his shot.

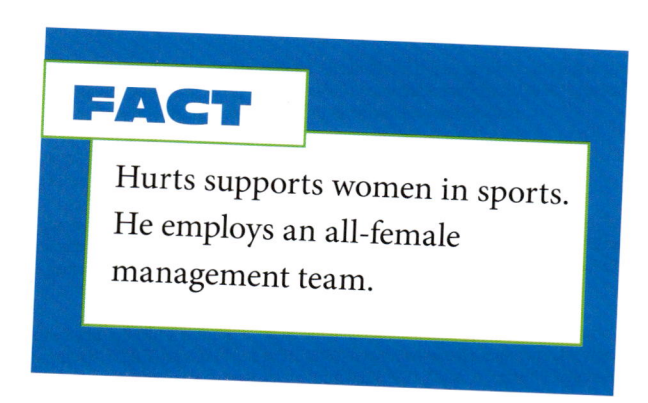

FACT

Hurts supports women in sports. He employs an all-female management team.

Combine Conclusion

At the NFL Combine, Hurts was rated "good backup with the potential to develop into starter." His strengths included his tremendous leadership skills, **poise**, toughness, and athletic ability. His weaknesses included patience when allowing routes to develop and sustaining rhythm as a passer.

19

On December 13, 2020, Hurts shredded the New Orleans Saints. He rushed for 106 yards. He also threw a touchdown pass as the Eagles won 24–21. They went on to lose the final three games of the season. Still, the coaches saw enough in Hurts to name him the starter for 2021.

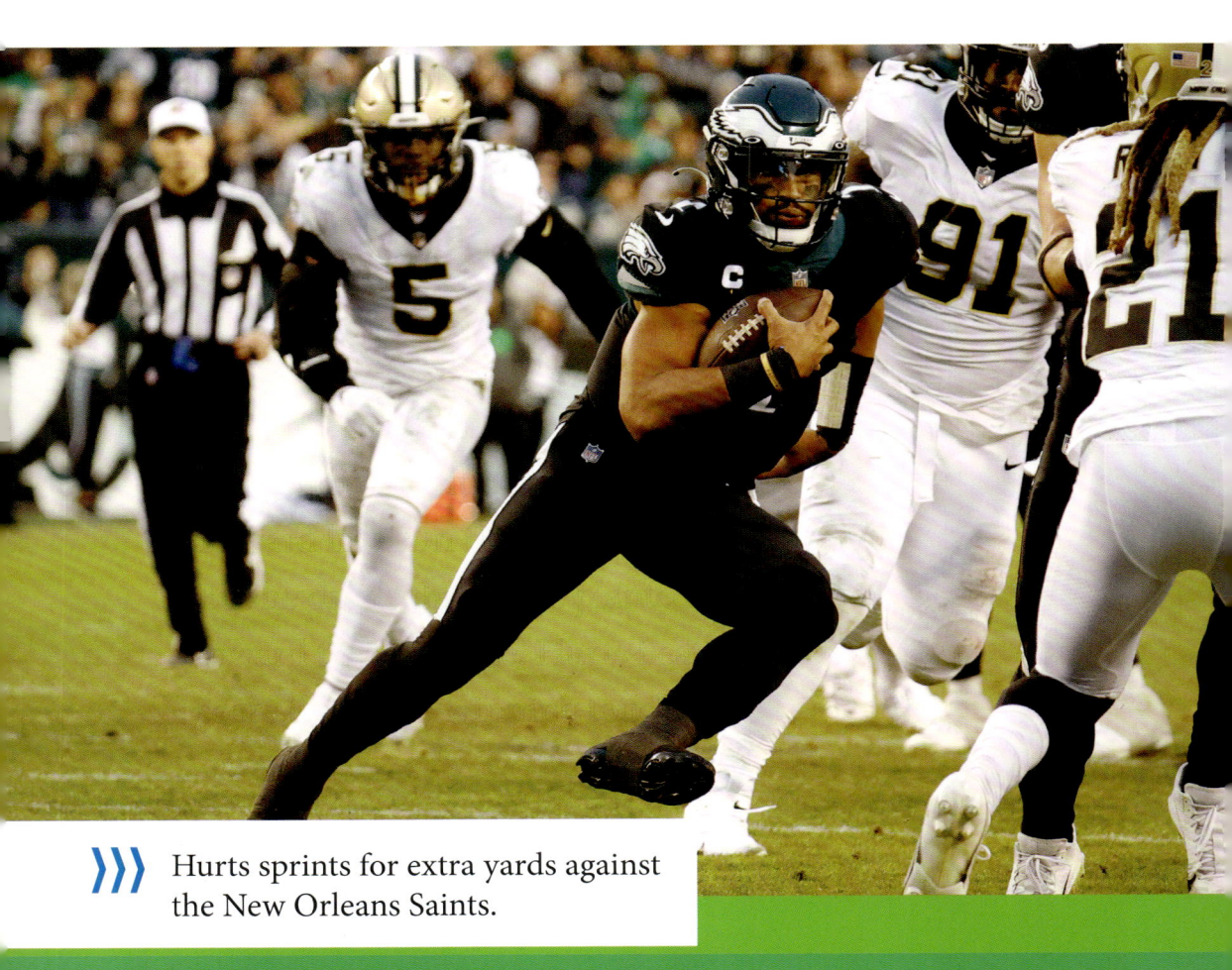

Hurts sprints for extra yards against the New Orleans Saints.

During the 2021 season, Hurts showed the world he was more than ready to be a starting quarterback in the NFL. While he had his ups and downs, the Eagles went 9–8 and made the playoffs.

Hurts rode that momentum into the 2022 season. He now had a full year of experience as a starter. Fans had high expectations, and Hurts delivered. He led the Eagles to a 14–3 record. Even better, he led his team to the Super Bowl. Although they didn't win, the standard was set.

The team was rolling at 10–1 during the 2023 season. But then, everything fell apart. They lost six of their last seven games. The Eagles went 11–6 and lost to Tampa Bay in the Wild Card game.

The Eagles came back big in the 2024 season, going 14–3 during the regular season. Hurts's dual-threat **capability** played a huge role in the team's success. His leadership and poise under pressure took the Eagles back to the Super Bowl.

CHAPTER FOUR

SUPERBOWL
HIGHS AND LOWS

On February 12, 2023, the Eagles faced the Kansas City Chiefs in Super Bowl LVII. The Eagles were favored, but not by much. The game went back and forth all four quarters.

Hurts delivered one of the greatest performances in Super Bowl history. He dominated the Kansas City defense. He threw for 304 yards and a touchdown. He rushed for 70 yards and three touchdowns. But with eight seconds left, the Chiefs kicked a field goal to win the game. The final score was 38–35.

FACT

Hurts holds the NFL record for the most rushing yards by a quarterback in Super Bowl history.

>>> Hurts scores a touchdown in the Super Bowl against Kansas City.

On February 9, 2025, the Eagles once again faced the Chiefs in the Super Bowl. This time, the Chiefs were favored. They were looking to win their third Super Bowl in a row, a **feat** which had never been done before.

And thanks to Hurts's master class performance, it still hasn't been done. Hurts broke his own Super Bowl rushing record with 72 yards. He passed for 221 yards and two touchdowns. This time, the game wasn't even close. The Eagles dominated the Chiefs, winning 40–22.

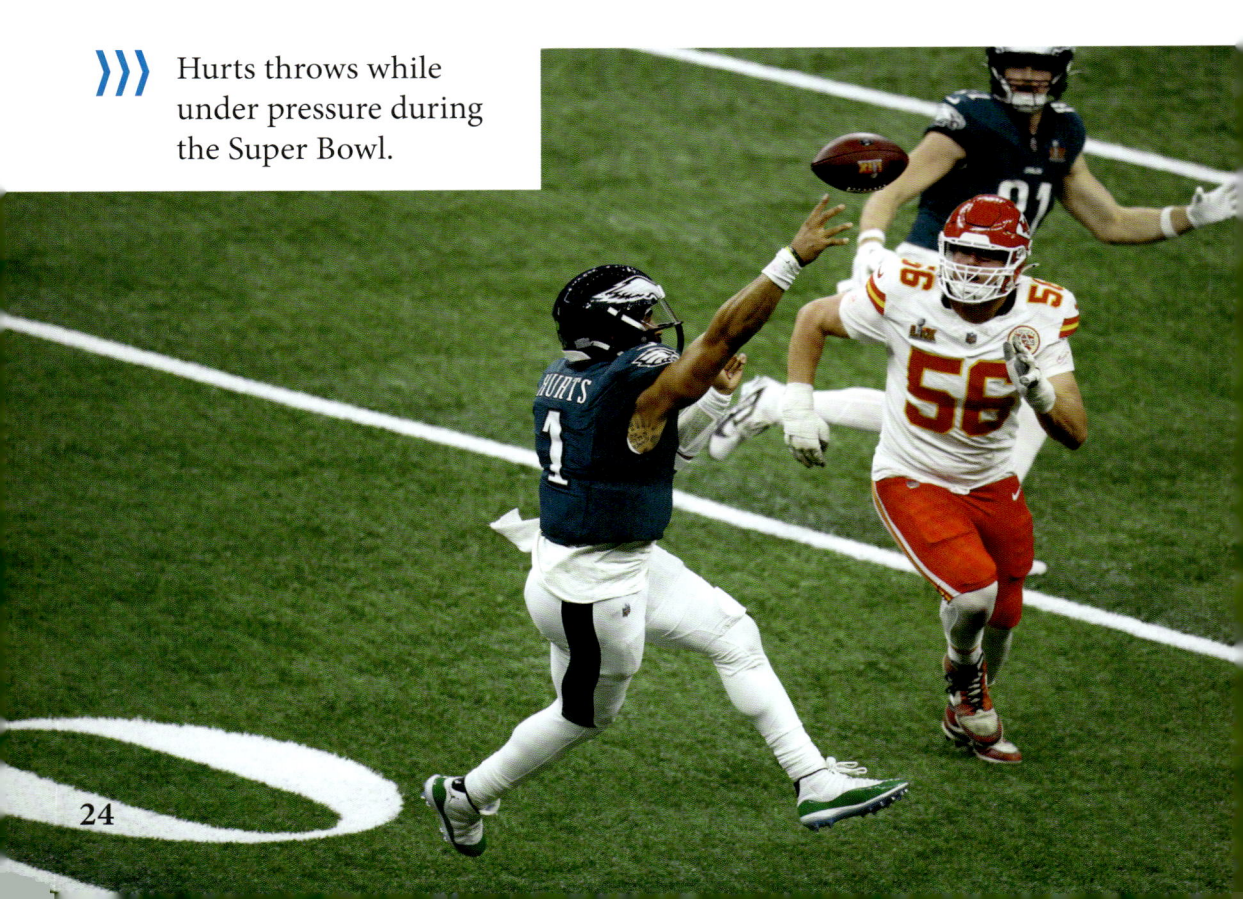

》》 Hurts throws while under pressure during the Super Bowl.

The Eagles were Super Bowl champs, and Jalen Hurts was the Super Bowl MVP.

"Things come right on time. The last time around, it wasn't our time, it wasn't my time and sometimes you have to accept that you have to wait your turn," said Hurts.

CHAPTER FIVE

BEYOND THE GAME

Hurts launched The Jalen Hurts Foundation in 2024. It supports children in need throughout Philadelphia. Hurts regularly visits schools and hospitals. He uses his fame and talent to inspire children to follow their dreams.

 Hurts (center) with members of his foundation

》》》 Hurts pauses to pray before a 2023 game.

"I was once a kid with a big dream. I was once a kid that had goals," Hurts said during a 2022 interview. "I just think the importance of knowing that to achieve those things, it's hard to do alone."

Hurts is very close to his family and has a strong Christian faith. He says both play a big part in why he has been so successful in the NFL.

FACT

Hurts set aside $70,000 to help cover his younger sister's college education.

Hurts has overcome a lot of **adversity**. He was benched at Alabama and fought back. He suffered a heartbreaking loss in a Super Bowl and fought back to win a Super Bowl. He has set records with his legs. He has electrified crowds with his arm. And he has done all of this in his twenties. If Hurts can stay healthy, who knows what else is in store for his football career.

》》》 During the third quarter of Super Bowl LIX in New Orleans, Hurts pulls back to launch a pass.

TIMELINE

1998 Born August 7 in Houston, Texas

2015 Commits to play college football at Alabama

2016 Named SEC Offensive Player and Freshman Prayer of the Year

2018 Wins NCAA title with the Alabama Crimson Tide

2019 Transfers to Oklahoma to finish college career

2020 Drafted by the Philadelphia Eagles

2020 Goes 1–3 as a starter over final four games in rookie season

2021 Named starting quarterback for the Eagles

2021 Leads Eagles to the playoffs in first season as starter

2022 Loses Super Bowl LVII to the Kansas City Chiefs, 38–35

2022 Selected to his first Pro Bowl (with another nod in 2023)

2023 Signs five-year, $255 million contract with the Eagles

2024 Launches The Jalen Hurts Foundation

2025 Wins Super Bowl LIX against the Kansas City Chiefs, 40–20

2025 Named MVP of Super Bowl LIX

GLOSSARY

ADVERSITY (add-VER-suh-tee)—difficulty or misfortune

CAPABILITY (kay-puh-BIL-i-tee)—a noteworthy achievement

FEAT (FEET)—a noteworthy achievement

GODFATHER (GOD-fah-thur)—a man who plays a role of leadership or responsibility in a child's life

GRUELING (GROOL-ing)—very difficult

REDEMPTION (ruh-DEM-shun)—making up for a previous error or defeat

RIVAL (RYE-vuhl)—a team or player who has a competitive history with another team or player

ROOKIE (RUH-kee)—first-year player in a professional sports league

POISE (POIZ)—self-confident and dignified

POWERLIFTING (POU-er-lif-ting)—a competition involving three tests of strength, including the bench press, squat, and dead lift

VETERAN (VE-truhn)—person with experience

VINTAGE (VIN-tij)—classic and recognizable

READ MORE

Berglund, Bruce. *Football GOATS: The Greatest Athletes of All Time.* North Mankato, MN: Capstone, 2022.

Klepeis, Alicia Z. *Philadelphia Eagles.* Minneapolis: Bellwether Media, 2024.

Zweig, Eric. *It's a Numbers Game!: Football.* Washington, D.C.: National Geographic Partners, 2022.

INTERNET SITES

Jalen Hurts Facts
kids.kiddle.co/Jalen_Hurts

Philadelphia Eagles: Jalen Hurts
philadelphiaeagles.com/team/players-roster/jalen-hurts

Sports Illustrated Kids: Football
sikids.com/football

INDEX

AUTHOR BIO

Matt Chandler is the author of more than 60 books for children and thousands of articles published in newspapers and magazines. He writes mostly nonfiction books with a focus on sports, ghosts and haunted places, and graphic novels. Matt lives in New York.